GW00362765

published by

stone soup

stone soup

Published by stone soup
stone soup, the fishergate centre, 4 fishergate, york, yo10 4fb, england
www.stone-soup.co.uk

First published in Great Britain by stone soup in 2001
Copyright © stone soup, york 2001
Text Copyright © stone soup, york 2001
First Edition · Second Impression - 2002

ISBN: 0-9541798-0-3

Illustrations by Pablo · www.muycollective.com

Printed and bound in England by Peter Turpins Associates, York

an introduction...

So what's a "100% True"?

Easy.

It's an insistent little thought virus which says nothing of value, and does nothing of use, but is cleverly coated in the easy to swallow camouflage of a low-brow, all-appealing base humour.

This means its pointless existence is perpetuated in a hundred pub conversations and it spreads like a sneaky brain germ.

Through your laughter and idle chatter it will gain a life of its own...

KEY TO ENTRIES:

YOU - Yes, we're spreading your little foibles out for the whole world to see. These are the secret brain-thoughts and quirks that you thought no-one knew about...

OTHERS - The odd habits, strange deeds and pointless activities of everyone who isn't you.

HOME - Locking your front door and drawing your curtains is no escape from our dogged truth probe. In this category we poke fun at things to do with home life, TV, parents and other cosy stuff.

here are 100% Trues about everything.
he key below forms a crude categorized
tructure into which they can all be
oughly crammed...

WORK - Surrounded by humming fans, buzzing screens and loaf-haired, ridiculous women in charge of the stationary cupboard, sometimes the only thing to do in an office is laugh at stupid truisms.

GOING OUT - Whether it's eating out, pints, cigarettes, getting served or crisps this category nails those mildly amusing things that ALWAYS happen when you're out and about.

CHILDHOOD - Where it all begins. A selection of 100% Trues which take in the whole gamut of being a kid - grazed knees, pencil cases and bouncy balls.

MOLES

Moles are always smaller
than you imagine.

FAT GIRL

At the end of every party
there's a fat girl crying.

TOILET SYNCHRONISATION

One of the most awkward things
that can happen in a pub is getting
your toilet to pint cycle synchronised
with a complete stranger.

GREEN CRISPS

You're never quite sure whether
it's ok to eat green crisps.

11

55378008

Everyone who grew up in the 80's will
have entered the number 55378008
into their calculator.

READING

Reading when you're drunk is horrible.

HOLLOW BEAR

You never stop being disappointed
that your chocolate bear is hollow.

POST OFFICE

It's impossible to feel sexy
in a post office.

BRUSHING YOUR TEETH

It feels wrong to be wearing
a coat whilst you brush your teeth.

WELLIES

You're always scared when you
put on another person's wellies.

SHARPENING A PENCIL

Sharpening a pencil with a knife
makes you feel really manly.

BLACK EYE

Whenever you see a woman
with a black eye you assume
she's been beaten up.

SPARE CHAIRS

You can't resist charging a 'comedy' amount of money for a spare chair when someone in a pub asks you 'is anyone sitting here?'

GUESS WHO?

Everybody knows someone who
looks a bit like a character
from Guess Who?

PLUGS

Some plugs are really
difficult to pull out.

'RACER' POSITION

It's never been cool to ride a bike
using the lower handlebars in
the 'racer' position.

FIRES

You're never quite sure whether it's against the law or not to have a fire in your back garden.

PLASTIC DOLLS

Whatever your age the desire
to make plastic dolls shag
is almost impossible to resist.

CUP-A-SOUP

Nobody dares make
cup-a-soup in a bowl.

APPLE

You never know where to look
when eating an apple.

27

WET CAT

It's impossible to describe
the smell of a wet cat.

OLD WOMEN

A lot of old women look like John Cleese
dressed as an old woman.

SPASH DOOLEY ICK NOO

Pretending to know a foreign language
that no one else understands
is a childhood rite of passage.

ADVERT

If ITV and Channel 4 are showing
the same advert you'll not be able to
resist rapidly switching between them.

POSH HOUSE

As a kid, you always had a friend
whose house smelt posh.

BROWN SUGAR

The request of brown sugar in tea
always causes a raised eyebrow.

TAKING SIDES

You know you're old when you take the side of a parent telling a child off in the street.

CUDDLY

A fat person in a lonely hearts
ad describing themselves as
'cuddly' fools no one.

DENTIST

It's not them fiddling about in your mouth that scares you at the Dentists. It's that secret code they speak in.

FUNNY BONE

Despite doing it almost daily as
a kid, as an adult you hardly ever
bang your funny bone.

CAR BOOT SALE

You're always suspicious of people who sell 'new things' at a car boot sale.

VIDEO CAMERA

Walking around with a video camera and doing a 'narration' makes you put on an unnaturally slow and deep voice. As if doing so will make 'and here's the cat' sound more impressive.

PRODDING

Prodding a fire with a stick
makes you feel manly.

BOUNCY BALL

Rummaging through an
overgrown garden will always
turn up a bouncy ball.

ONE-NIGHT STAND

For a girl sometimes the only deciding factor in whether to have a one night stand is how shaved her legs are.

UGLY

Every so often you see
an ugly version of yourself.

STROKING HORSES

You're always a bit scared
when you stroke a horse.

DOG

You'll always remember the day a dog ran into your school.

'MUM' OR 'DAD'

The single most embarrassing thing
you can do as a schoolchild is to
call your teacher 'Mum' or 'Dad'.

MONKEY

The smaller the monkey, the
more it looks like it would kill
you at the first given opportunity.

FAT FINGERS

Fat fingers look dirtier than thin ones.

SANDY LEGS

No pain or trauma is comparable to
when you had sand rubbed off
your legs by your parents.

CUSTARD CREAMS

Plenty of people claim to have eaten
the biscuit around a custard cream
whilst keeping the filling intact.
But you've never actually
seen them do it.

CONTACT LENSES

Everyone who wears contact
lenses has got a horror story.

FOOTBALL CHANT

At the end of a football chant you always get that sad tailing off as three people try and sing a second verse. Only to realise the moment has passed.

SHRUG

It's quite difficult to remember
the last time you shrugged.

FELT-TIP PENS

When using felt-tip pens for the first time in ages you realise you'd forgotten about these really annoying rolled up tiny bits of paper that get dragged around whatever you are colouring in.

CRUTCHES

Some days you see a lot of people on crutches.

DRAWING A BICYCLE

When drawing a bicycle you will
not, for the life of you, be able to
figure out how the seat is attached.

OLD PEOPLE'S HIPS

As they are surely intended to
be quite an important part of your
body it makes no sense at all that
old people's hips break so often.

MILK

Very occasionally your body
'must have milk'.

OWL

No one you know knows
what owl tastes like.

TEXT MESSAGING

At every party they'll be a bloke
text messaging his girlfriend.

FLUSH

During a toilet visit the majority
of blokes like to pull the chain
halfway through and then
'race against the flush'.

MAGPIE

Neither you, nor anybody you
know, has ever had anything
stolen by a Magpie.

'DYNASTY'

Opening double doors with both hands
makes you feel a bit 'Dynasty'.

MOBILE PHONES

Old women with mobile
phones look wrong.

FRISBEE

It's impossible to look cool
whilst picking up a frisbee.

'A BIT OF A LAWYER'

Some situations crop up
where everyone
'is a bit of a lawyer'.

TUNNEL

Driving through a tunnel
makes you feel excited.

DOMINO RALLY

People don't seem to do those
huge domino rally things nearly
as much as they used to.

SQUIRRELS

You never see baby squirrels.

PACKET OF FAGS

Finding a packet of fags
makes your night.

LIMP

Having days where you pretend to
limp is an important childhood ritual.

EYE CONTACT

You'll occasionally spend a whole
night unintentionally making
eye contact with a complete stranger.

MYRA

You don't meet many
people called Myra.

MOBILE PHONE 2

It's very difficult to use
someone else's mobile phone.

EATING OUT

Whenever you eat out with a group of
friends someone will make the 'shall
we leave without paying' joke.

SALT

You never run out of salt.

FAMILY FORTUNES

You'll never meet anyone who
is one of the hundred people
surveyed by Family Fortunes.

HILL ROLLING

Thanks to small rocks, odd angles
and dog pooh, rolling down a hill
is never anything like you
imagine it'll be.

CROSSING THE ROAD

You can tell a lot about a person
from the way they cross a road.

NAME BADGES

Despite assistants in large stores all wearing badges you feel really patronising if you refer to them by name.

COUPLES

Couples who have just fallen in love
walk slower than everybody else.

OLD LADIES

Old ladies can eat
more than you think.

BATHROOM TAP

Water from the bathroom tap tastes better than water from the kitchen tap.

BROWN PAPER BAG

Carrying your shopping in
a brown paper bag makes you
feel all American.

ANCHOVIES

Most people learn about
anchovies from a pizza menu.

DIRECTIONS

When you ask for directions people always give you about 50 seconds worth too much.

POSH SHOPPING

If you shop somewhere posh
you feel you have to move slowly.

'BONK'

It's only tabloid newspapers
that actually use the word 'bonk'.

GOTH MEN

Goth men walk more upright
than normal people.

DOG CARRYING

You can't respect a man
who carries a dog.

JIMMY HILL

Everyone thinks it was their school that
invented the classic childhood insult
of rubbing their chin and saying
'Chinny rack on' or similar.

EYESIGHT

If you mention your eyesight people
will try and persuade you that
theirs is worse.

STUCK

There's no panic like the panic you
momentarily feel when you think
you've got your hand or head
stuck in something.

COAT HANGERS

No one knows the origins
of their wire coat hangers.

GENITALS

Friends always insist that their
dog is 'just playing' when it comes
and attacks your genitals.

LETTUCE

By inserting lettuce you
convince yourself you've just
made a sandwich healthy.

SWANS

Despite constant warnings from people,
you've never met anybody who has
had their arm broken by a swan.

SMELLY FIELD

Driving past a smelly field compels
you to make the 'who farted' joke.

MISSING INGREDIENTS

Whenever you compliment your mother on a splendid meal she'll insist it could have been better if she hadn't forgotten some completely random and pointless ingredient.

HANGOVER CLOTHES

Whilst suffering from a hangover and getting dressed you'll discover clothes you never knew you had.

PLUGS 2

The most painful household incident
is wearing socks and stepping
on an upturned plug.

CAR DOORS

People who don't drive
slam car doors too hard.

NEW JERSEY

You can't see the words 'New Jersey' without saying 'Noo Joisey'.

COLDS

Colds disappear when
you're in the bath.

OPENING LETTERS

Opening your house's previous
occupant's letters leaves you with
the nagging feeling that one day
you'll be found out.

SKATEBOARDER

You never actually see a street
skateboarder land a trick.

STEREO

The radio is the last thing to
go wrong on a stereo.

THREE CHORDS

People who can only play three chords
on the guitar shouldn't bother telling
and really don't need to prove it.

STIRRING PAINT

You've turned into your dad the day
you put aside a thin piece of wood
to specifically stir paint with.

COMPUTER SOUND EFFECTS

Whenever someone uses a computer on a TV programme it is followed by a loud and unrealistic sound effect.

PETS

Other people's pets have no manners.

NICKNAMES

If you catch the bus every day you always end up giving fellow regulars nicknames you wouldn't want them to know about.

FALLING OVER

Some days you just know you're going to fall over.

UNCLE

Everyone had an uncle who
tried to steal their nose.

BRICKS

Bricks are horrible to carry.

CHIPS

In every plate of chips
there is a bad chip.

INSECTS

Other countries' insects
are really frightening.

HANDWRITING

Sometimes you don't write
in your own handwriting.

SANDWICHES

Triangle sandwiches taste
better than square ones.

DRUMS

When you pretend to play the drums
you'll always cross your hands.

120

BALLOON

Beneath every floating balloon
there is a tearful child.

stone soup

Compiled by Tom Sharp, Andy Milson & Thom Craigen
with help from: Matt Bennett, Anna Cook, Justin Jamieson,
Jackal, Chris Walker, Hemma, Mojo, Jo, John Probemeister,
Joe G, Amber, Sam Flannery, Simon Daubney, Sarah Read,
Helen Batty, Colin Bridgeman, Wayne Field, Caroline Blanckley,
Andrew Peplow and Sue Milson.

Share your 100% True! with the world!

www.100true.com

Leave your 100% True! ideas
and rate other people's online.

You can also sign up for our
FREE monthly email of new favourites...